PEOPLE DEVELOPMENT:

THE BEST PART OF LEADING A TEAM

Jim Bohn, Ph.D.

Jim Bohn, PhD is an author and researcher-practitioner focused on improving organizational performance one person at a time. Dr. Bohn has decades of on-the-job experience in addition to a strong foundation of academic training. This book represents his deep interest in ensuring people find satisfaction in their jobs.

People Development: The Best Part of Leading a Team

ProAxios Publications

Cover design by Brian Holz - Atomic Design

Editing and interior design by Emerald Books

Publication Date: February 2023

ISBN-9798377800750

PEOPLE DEVELOPMENT:

THE BEST PART OF LEADING A TEAM

Jim Bohn, Ph.D.

CONTENTS

Chapter 5

Creating the Conditions for Motivation

Motivation is a big and important subject. We review five common motivations, then outline detailed actions we can take to develop people. We evaluate some scenarios to discover how to activate employee motivation.

Chapter 6

Shallow Water or Deep Water?

We look at a significant list of potential development activities and categorize them as more or less complex, individual-based or team-based. Shallow water is for lesser experienced team members, while deep water is for those with the capacity to handle complex situations.

Chapter 7

The Development Zone

The rubric in this chapter is intended to give leaders a framework for considering where, when, and how much to invest in an employee. We start with the basics of relationship and trust, then consider how the development activity will benefit the organization.

Chapter 8

Overcoming Hindrances to Employee Development

Though it is essential for success, employee development is not always easy. We evaluate obstacles from the employee, the manager, and the organization. We reveal one critical element of managerial behavior that makes all the difference.

Chapter 9

The Power of Leadership Patience in Developing Others

Leadership patience is not often addressed in leadership literature, but patience is essential during development because new things don't always go as planned, and a leader's reaction makes a difference in how the development activity will be received and integrated into a person's work life.

Chapter 10

Thinking about How We Think

Teaching people how we think is an incredibly valuable development activity. It's worth the time to teach people how we think. The Cognitive Apprenticeship model clarifies how to approach this element of development. It simply means expressing how we think about how we think!

Chapter 11

Leadership Is More than a Job

We summarize what we've learned and the look forward to the road ahead, including recommendations for academic research.

DEDICATION

For Elizabeth Joy,

"Wiz"
My daughter, friend, and oftentimes counselor.
Juris Doctor.
The ultimate people person.
Though you left us too soon,
You changed the world.
Love you more than pancakes,

Dad

NOTE FROM THE AUTHOR

The goal of the book is to provide organizational leaders with a guide to analyze how they develop people, ultimately improving the process and enhancing the lives of others in the workplace.

This handbook is intentionally short and direct. Leaders are busy, and they like to cut to the chase. When it comes to development, leaders get a lot of "how to," but very little "why." It's often more about getting the job done than why we do the job in the first place. My primary intention in this book is to give leaders a *why* for people development because most of the time, development is another organizational check-the-box activity that lacks meaning.

I've intentionally spent extra time on the *why* because we don't often think about the rationale for development. I believe as leaders we have an innate sense of the *why*, but articulating it clearly is crucial for activating our own motivation.

Development has the power to transform people and organizations. Figuring out the *why* gives our efforts a focus. I provide straightforward and concrete actions to take in the day-to-day involvement with teams. I address some common objections to development and point out specific leadership behaviors that make development stick.

Development is a critical part of leading people, so it requires a framework for thinking. To date, there is no commonly understood theory of employee development. In this book, I've provided a definition of development and added different aspects of the process, focusing on the responsibility of the employee and leader.

Judgment is required in people development, and this book will increase your capacity to make effective judgments about who, how and when to develop. So, take this deep dive with me, and then consider how to transform your development intentions into reality.

According to many professionals, people development is the key to employee retention and engagement, especially during this current season of quiet quitting. In other words, if people feel like they are developing, they're likely to stay with an employer. This book is an attempt to answer the need.

Ultimately, people development requires an attitude of delight in the success of others. As Elizabeth Thelen says, "We don't have to do this; we *get* to do this." As a leader, you can make that choice and impact your people right now...for the rest of their careers.

And maybe you'll change their lives along the way.

—Jim Bohn, Ph.D.

Jenna's Story

Jenna Smith walked into Valeria Channing's office. They had an appointment for 9:00 a.m. When she arrived, Valeria, her boss, said, "Come on in. So great to see you this morning."

But Jenna was looking up at the ceiling and did not sit down at Valeria's desk. She was uncharacteristically withdrawn and disconnected.

"What's up?" asked Valeria, puzzled by Jenna's demeanor.

"Well, I wanted to be professional and let you know I'm leaving Hodges Manufacturing. Here's my letter of resignation."

Wide-eyed, Valeria pushed her chair back from her desk. Jenna was one of her best team members with significant skills in accounting and I.T. Jenna was highly respected, and Valeria knew others could follow. "Why are you leaving? Our team has been very successful. We've done some great things together."

"There are good people on this team, but I feel like I've wasted my time the past eighteen months."

Valeria squinted. "What do you mean?"

"Well, I'm in exactly the same place I was back then. I haven't learned anything new, and the challenge isn't what it was. I've done my job, but nothing has changed for me. I don't see any prospects for promotion. I want to grow in my career and gain more experience."

"Well, surely we could work something out. There are lots of new projects and opportunities coming down the pike in the next few months. Won't you reconsider?"

"I'm sorry. My mind is made up, and I have a new job waiting. Just wanted you to know. I've enjoyed working with you, but I need more."

Jenna's story is not unusual, but her exit could have been avoided. Jenna wanted her days to count; she wanted to learn and have challenging experiences; in short, she wanted to be developed. And Valeria had not anticipated Jenna's need for development.

Elizabeth Thelen reminds us that "feeling underutilized can be a tough place for an individual."

Bob's Story

Bob Cramer had been a payroll clerk for Hutchinson Industries for thirty-five years. He was glad to put in time and enjoy his boat on the weekends. For him, a job was simply a paycheck, and he was content with that. Bob was a dependable worker, but he only did what was needed. He was running out the clock for his retirement, which was seven years away.

Through a corporate merger, Bob was transferred (unwillingly) to a new division. His new boss, Angie Martinez, knew he had more to offer, and she needed to increase his productivity for the sake of the team. With the increased workload, she needed all her team members to operate at 100%.

Angie's development challenge was to increase Bob's output. She had to activate Bob's natural motivations, so he could learn more and contribute more to the team.

Lisa's Story

Fresh out of university, Lisa Magnuson had a full head of steam to change the world. Entering a large corporation, she was overwhelmed by things she hadn't experienced in her classes, including politics and the intense pace of the work.

The challenge for her boss, Gordon Zahn, was to effectively develop her without overwhelming her, to ensure Lisa found enough challenge without giving up. Helping her navigate the corporate environment would be a key element of her development activity. Gordon had a wonderful opportunity to make her successful, both near- and long-term, and to ensure Lisa would gain some tenacity along the way.

Do any of these stories sound familiar?

These are common challenges in development.

* **Leaders** need a way of thinking to improve their employee development efforts.

* **Organizations** need some clear principles for creating development opportunities.

* **HR teams** need a framework for guiding and training leaders how to develop people--not just expecting the boxes to be checked.

* **Employees** need leaders and managers who can create development opportunities (and ultimately build other leaders!).

The point is this: There is a significant need for People Development across a career, and leaders need a framework to guide them.

Let's begin at the beginning.

LET'S BE HONEST: ISN'T DEVELOPMENT JUST ANOTHER BOX I HAVE TO CHECK?

Whenever I ask someone how they're doing and they respond with a sarcastic, "Living the dream" or "Same old, same old" I know something about their work situation. They're either not challenged enough or they're simply bored. Both of those conditions can be changed by a leader who takes the time and effort to develop them.

Question 6 of the famous Q12 Employee Engagement survey asks: "Is there someone at work who encourages your *development*?" With a yes or no answer, an employee is supposed to address a key part of their work life. It's a fair question, but how would that work in practice? Is anyone at their job truly interested in their development?

As both a manager and an employee, sitting down to write out an employee development plan for myself was *very low* on my list of priorities. It was one more corporate thing to do. I had little enthusiasm for the process.

From a corporate standpoint, we leaders rarely discussed why we did this annual work of filling out a development form. We just had to comply with HR protocol. And even though we intuitively knew there was more to development, we sometimes felt like were just checking a box.

But along the way, I discovered that investing in people was a completely different matter. I got excited when I thought about how to encourage someone in a new opportunity and support them as they learned. I got even more excited when I thought about how that experience would benefit them down the road, both in the organization and possibly years (decades?) into the future.

The formal process was uninteresting. Sometimes it caused me to wonder why I was even doing this. Conversely, the one-on-one interactions of development were deeply motivating.

Because when I worked with my team, I got fired up about what I could do to make their lives richer and better in the workplace. I found deep satisfaction in creating an environment where they could become stronger and more capable team members.

People development was the answer.

The notion that I could do more than just manage people energized me. I realized I could add something to their lives by taking an interest in their long-term success. It was neat to see people expand their abilities and take on greater things. It mattered to them, and it mattered to me.

How do we train managers to develop people?

Managers go through extensive training in executive leadership or high-potential programs. At what point do we truly give them insight into developing people? At what point do they sit with a group of peers and ask, "What success have you had developing people? What process did you use? What worked and what didn't? What did you do to get people interested in the development process?"

At what point do we activate deep motivation to build our team's strength by focusing on the development of people? Executive development commonly provides skills managing teams and improving financial analysis for the sake of corporate output, but people development, a key component, doesn't seem to be included in training.

The purpose of this book is to take a closer look at employee development—why we do it and what it takes to do it *well*. We also consider the process for the benefit of our companies and our team members.

How do we develop the next generation of leaders? Their expectations for development are very high. What's our plan to meet that expectation?

What about the impact of the pandemic?

"I feel that leaders have become distracted by their daily responsibilities on top of the new challenges brought on by the pandemic. It's easier to hire someone from the outside and see what they can get rather than develop someone from the inside."

—Carrie Lauersdorf, Engineer

As we've discussed, the primary organizational goal that comes to mind is **retention of the best people.**

By strengthening the ranks through good development, we:

* ***increase*** the likelihood of organizational success (By remaining with an organization over time, people understand the nuances of their company and are able to use that knowledge for the benefit of everyone.),

* ***reduce*** recruitment costs, and

* ***improve*** the speed of organizational decision-making because of the knowledge built up and retained by long-term employees.

The Practical Benefit of Developing Others: There's an ROI for the Leader

We often discuss the need to retain the best people. Fact is, employees will deliver results for leaders who have demonstrated they are interested in their long-term development. People sense that you believe developing them is more than a job; they know when you show that their development is a *calling*.

So, build the ROI! Get your people engaged in the development process, and make it work for *them*, for *you*, and for the *organization*!

* Are you simply throwing projects at your team members or truly considering which efforts will develop them over the long haul?

* Have you talked directly to them about the value of the development experiences you're sending their way?

When employees know your development plan stretches out over the long haul, they understand you are mindful of them not only as employees, but as people who want to learn and increase their own value to the team. You're looking out for them. *And that increases loyalty to you and retention to the corporation.*

Jay Held compares employee development to an ROI:

"The investment in the types of development plans you discuss is that as your people become better developed, the success of the team and of you as a leader grows exponentially."

Take some time and write down what you believe about people development.

ORGANIZATIONAL CONTEXT

The components of employee development are: (1) the organizational context, including HR support for the goals of the corporation—an essential reason why we develop employees is to accomplish organizational goals; (2) the employee need for development; (3) the leader, and; (4) the development experience itself.

Each of these merits personal reflection and analysis.

Organizational context is critical because it provides funding, support from other leaders, and support from key teams like HR. Without organizational support, even the best development intentions fail.

The employee's desire for development is their motivation to get better at their role and enhance their career.

The leader is the coordinator of action for the employee in the context of the organization. The leader requires a framework and skillset to create thoughtful development based on the individual as well as help creating opportunities to get the experience or make critical connections.

The development experience is the specific activity, project, or opportunity the employee engages in to achieve long-term learning.

CHAPTER 1 SYNOPSIS

Employee retention is the outcome of good development. Leaders (and organizations) need a method for developing people that doesn't just check the box. Training managers to truly develop people will take employees beyond a formal annual requirement, and good development has a return on investment for the leader and their team. We've also examined the components of people development.

Let's move on to a formal definition of people development.

PEOPLE DEVELOPMENT

WHAT IS DEVELOPMENT?

Employee development is critical for employee retention. It's a fact. So how do we develop people? What are our *motives* for development? What are some *means* of development? What do people *need*? What are practical things we can do to develop people? And, most important, what should we focus on with each team member?

We *know* that hiring a new employee after a valued team member has moved on is very expensive, both in terms of financial and time investment. It costs money to lose people and find their replacements. (It can also have a dramatic impact on team morale.)

Important! Developing organizational strength costs less and requires less risk than taking on someone new.

* An entry-level employee turnover costs between 30% and 50% of their annual salary to replace.

* A mid-level employee turnover costs 150% and above of their annual salary to replace.

* A high-level or highly specialized employee costs approximately 400% of their annual salary to replace.[1]

---

1 Simply Benefits. (2021, October 7). Employee retention - what is the true cost of losing an employee? Simply Benefits. www.simplybenefits.ca/blog/employee-retention-what-is-the-true-cost-of-losing-anemployee

We know that employee retention comes from employee satisfaction. Employees reflect on their relative happiness with the following questions: *Does my leader create opportunities for me to gain knowledge and experience that enhances my current role and creates opportunities for future roles and promotion? Do my days at this workplace count for my long-term success?*

We also know recent generations are more vocal about their personal development. They want their leadership to be involved in their growth, enhancing their skills and abilities. Bottom line? Development is *not* optional!

Barry Keller says, "I think all generations have wanted development. In my opinion, the worker shortage has given younger generations leverage to push for things other generations either didn't think they could get or didn't have the courage to ask for. And now older generations are reaping the benefits as well."

Is development growth?

Sometimes we hear the word *growth* in the context of development, but to me that word is vague. Development and growth are *similar* but not the same in the workplace, so let's clarify with some working definitions.

Growth means learning from experience and gaining insight, understanding, and discernment over time.

Development is focused specifically on our work and career experiences.

Growth is broadly personal; development is career-focused.

People development is NOT a career path nor career planning.

People development is not the same as a career path, though it may contribute to enhancing one's career. It is not a succession plan. It is not a series of actions to ensure promotion. It is not a guarantee of future opportunities.

It is an intentional investment to increase an employee's capacity and skills.

Developing a career path is something employees do for themselves. They know where they want to go, what they want to accomplish, and what they want to become. While managers may spend time discussing their career, it is rare to find a manager leading an employee through years of career planning. (And when we're honest, most career planning documents collect dust in a drawer somewhere.)

"From years of conversations, I have seen most people across all levels of the organization need help figuring out what's possible. They either don't know what opportunities are available or don't know how to figure out how to leverage their skills." —Barry Keller

That's where thoughtful development comes in.

Development actions and experiences are part of a career path but not the career path itself. Development actions don't always mean more money (at the time) or a higher position (at the time). So, it's critical that leaders communicate that not all development experiences will immediately turn into tangible gains.

Development and employee engagement go hand-in-hand.

Want to increase your employee engagement scores? Spend more time developing people. A fully developed workforce is more likely to feel a sense of engagement in their work, their team, and their organization because, by developing, they're bringing more of themselves to the work. As people develop, their motivation to contribute increases, accelerating a sense of employee engagement and satisfaction.

Critical caveat: There is no guaranteed cause and effect, but there is good practice and common sense.

Development is not a cause-and-effect, tried-and-true system. In other words, we don't naturally receive employee motivation (and retention) because we took the time to develop them. No system is foolproof and works 100% of the time. No matter. It's far better to have a system that guides us through a process and has a better chance of employee retention than doing nothing. And with that caveat, there are strong reasons to engage in employee development.

It's a myth that development costs a lot of money. It can be as simple as a thorough conversation.

Not all employee development means sending someone to an expensive workshop! Sometimes the best development experience is a manager sitting down with an employee. They might explain how they approached a problem in the past or provide a different perspective on how others might see the problem.

For example, organizational politics is one area where conversations are extremely valuable. Here's an opportunity for you to engage deeply with your team member around something called a cognitive apprenticeship. The term *cognitive apprenticeship* means helping another person learn by *describing how one thinks about a situation*. In other words, when a leader takes the time to explain how they think about a situation, an employee gains insights they might otherwise not have seen. Employees are keen to learn from experienced managers. "Teach me how to think about stuff. I want to learn your insights and the reason you use the approach you use." (We'll cover that in detail in a later chapter).

Why do people seek development?

It's simple, really. People spend a third of their lives at work, and they want that time to matter. Fundamentally, they want to make a living to support a family and accomplish their personal goals. But beyond those basic needs, people want to know they've *made a difference* in the world; they want to know *they mattered*; they want to know *they influenced others*; and they want to know they are *competent*. People want to be esteemed. These are basic motivations common to all human beings.

"Meaningful work is key to having an emotional connection to work, especially with the new generations of people entering the workforce."

—Mike Markiewicz, Executive Director of the UWM-Milwaukee Lubar School of Business

People want to learn new skills and increase their repertoire of career experiences. They want to enhance their likelihood of promotion. Overall, they want to increase their value as employees and enhance their self-respect through learning and experience.

The amount of time, effort, and sacrifice people spend on education, whether in trade school or university, compels them to seek a return on investment. In short, they want to know their effort benefited them in the long run. But formal education is only a beginning. We all know that. And having completed formal education, people want to expand their professional capabilities into the workforce. They want to become more.

At a very high level, employees seek development to:

1) Increase confidence and self-efficacy

2) Increase and deepen skills

3) Increase their chances of promotion

4) Gain visibility within the company

5) Add to their repertoire and resume, making them more valuable both internal to a company and externally, if they choose to leave for another job

6) Make their job interesting

When you think of your team members, which of these things is most important to them?

It's important to think about the rationale for development. Not all development is equal. Suzanne Sherry articulated a useful way to think about development:

Category	Addressing	Specifics
Performance	Performance deficit (gaps)	Person not meeting requirements of the job
On-the-job Development	Day-to-day issues that come up	How to deal with politics, addressing specific work issues, on-the-job training, stretch assignments, problem solving.
Development for the next job	Frustrations with current situation, level of engagement, desire for more money, career path	Leader needs to understand what's behind this call for development?

PEOPLE DEVELOPMENT: A DEFINITION

Let's consider a working definition of development. You likely have your own thoughts about the subject. This is a framework to help think through the goals of development.

PEOPLE DEVELOPMENT IS THE PROCESS OF

(1) gaining new knowledge,

(2) learning new skills,

(3) improving self-efficacy,

(4) strengthening existing capabilities, and

(5) gaining achievements that validate someone's value in the organization.

1. **Gaining new knowledge:** When someone's knowledge base is stagnant, they become bored and uninterested in work. New knowledge is always a good experience, and though it may be tough to acquire, there's a satisfaction in learning something new, whether it is technology or leadership psychology.

2. **Learning new skills**: One way for people to develop is to simply gain a new skill. It could be a new software package or improved speaking skills. It could be more complex, like learning to navigate politics. Learning something new always makes life more interesting and gets us off the hamster wheel of routine. Developing people gives them something new to work on, a challenge that increases their interest in their job and cuts boredom in the process. It is not unusual for people to coast when they're bored. *Organizations cannot afford people who coast.* Learning adds a sense of achievement, which is deeply gratifying. Learning also increases personal value in the workforce. Finally, learning is portable—you can take it with you!

3. **Improving self-efficacy:** Self-efficacy is a sense of control.[2] When we develop people, we want them to feel they control an outcome. This is more than simple confidence; it is a real capacity to assess a situation and discern whether they can achieve a desired outcome, no matter how complex. Essentially, increased self-efficacy means more confidence

---

2 Bandura, Self-Efficacy: The Exercise of Control, W. H. Freeman & Co (1997).

in complex situations. Self-efficacy builds strength for their next role. People know they can take on a greater challenge based on their accomplishments. When people deepen their self-efficacy, they increase their value in their organizations and enhance their own self-respect.

4. **Strengthening existing capabilities:** Sometimes people want to go deep on a subject or skill they already know, such as the accountant who wants to master a certain level of expertise to become certified, or the engineer who wants to strengthen his knowledge of physics. Some people don't want to be generalists, they want to be experts, validating their purpose (and reputation) in the workplace.

5. **Gaining achievements that validate someone's value in the organization:** When people work together to accomplish something big, they discover their value as part of an organization. When someone walks away from the success of a large project, they realize: *I learned, I contributed, I added value and expertise, I was part of something bigger than myself, and I'm proud to have worked with those people. I was a critical part of that success. I am valuable in this organization.* Achievements become reputations that increase the likelihood of visibility and promotions.

Now, each element of this definition requires on-the-ground efforts by leaders to ensure development takes place. They will be discussed later in this book.

Before we proceed, here's an opportunity for you to pause and reflect on what you're doing to develop others.

From your perspective, what is the value of developing people?

What is *your* process for developing others?

Is your employee development approach haphazard or systematic?

What successes have you seen over time when you apply effort to people development?

Bottom line: development adds satisfaction to work life.

It's a fact that good development means people are more likely to say, "This day was a great day for learning. I feel satisfied for what I've done. I have added something to my life, I have gained knowledge, and I have made a difference in my team, my company, and maybe the world." That's why people want development opportunities.

CHAPTER 2 SYNOPSIS

Development is not growth. It is not career planning, and there is no guarantee of cause and effect for leaders who take the time to develop people. People seek development for many reasons, but primarily to increase their value to themselves and their organizations. We reviewed a working definition of development.

Let's move on to leaders' motivation for developing others.

THE HIGH CALLING OF DEVELOPING PEOPLE

Development is more than a job,
and it's the best part of leading a team.

WORKING DEFINITION

People Development is the process of

(1) gaining new knowledge,

(2) learning new skills,

(3) improving efficacy,

(4) strengthening existing capabilities, and

(5) gaining achievements that validate
someone's value in the organization.

Developing people is a calling.

In moments of honest, private reflection, all of us struggle with the lifetime value of our work as leaders and managers. Why do we do what we do? Does it matter? As a leader, I have found deep personal satisfaction from truly developing people and watching them succeed. Developing people is a calling. If leaders are not interested in developing people, are they truly in the right role? With a four-decade perspective on leadership, and using servant leadership as a philosophical framework, I found that developing people had an immense impact not only on team members, but also on my own leadership satisfaction. I believe leaders will find value as they reflect on the incredible importance of the *calling* to develop others. The very fact that we get to do this is an amazing responsibility and privilege.

There is satisfaction in seeing others achieve their goals.

One of the unspoken reasons for developing other people is the satisfaction of seeing others accomplish their goals in life. Good leaders can see how development increases the strengths of their people and to achieve their goals. Ultimately, people development requires an attitude of delight in the success of others. As a leader, you can make that choice and impact people right now and for the rest of their careers. The smile on the face of someone who has accomplished a huge development goal is a priceless satisfaction for a leader.

Consider your people. How are you helping them achieve their goals right now?

Take the long view. Developing people is hard work. It takes time away from other projects, emails, conference calls, and the non-stop, day-to-day pressures of managing. Developing people requires thoughtful effort, consideration of each individual, and follow-through to ensure our development intentions turn into action. Taking the long view means understanding that people don't grow overnight. If we are frustrated with them ("Why can't you get this done?"), we are not developing them, we are using them. And they will quickly figure that out.

Consider your people. Do they know you're interested in their long-term development?

Developing others is its own reward. I had a team member who found it difficult to speak to large groups. It caused him some serious career challenges, and he became more and more anxious about addressing customers. Other leaders who he worked for simply pushed him to speak, and he failed. Together we developed a plan to get him some training in public speaking. It took time, persuasion, funding, and a few days away from the job, but it was essential. In the end, he told me it changed his life, giving him more confidence and removing a sense of failure.

Consider your leadership influence. Looking back, how did your development efforts help someone improve their career?

Understand your personal philosophical foundation for developing others. Have you considered why you do what you do as a leader? Clearly, your core skill set (finance, legal, accounting, operations, engineering, or human resources) is a valuable tool in your leadership toolbox, but how do you answer your own *why*? Is there a part of your mindful workspace that says, "I intentionally develop other people. I create paths for their success. I anticipate what they need. I find satisfaction in the achievements of others."?

**Consider your foundation for developing others.
What is your *why*?**

Reflect on the satisfaction of developing others.

Developing others is its own reward. Looking back over a career, I see people who I hired that have moved up, whose lives were better, who improved skills and gained motivational insights our mutual investment in their development. There is a deep satisfaction of knowing I helped someone else achieve great things.

*Developing others brings value to others
and enriches our lives as leaders.*

The Long Long-term Impact of Development: The Billiard Ball Effect

When we develop others, they invariably pick up skills and values from the work we do with them. There is an immense effect we cannot see, but we know it happens because of others who have developed us and whose influence changed our lives! We learned from others and have passed on knowledge, skills, and wisdom to the next generation of leaders, who in turn pass on some of those skills to those who follow! Our investment pays off down the road.

The value here? We often ask, "What happens if they leave?" But if they leave, they will take some of your influence with them, along with the fact that you took the time to make them a better employee. Our development investment lives on and influences the world.

And though we may feel the loss of a great employee, "it's not a bad thing to be an exporter of talent." (Mike Markiewicz)

"Former employees who leave happy can in future fill a role as corporate ambassadors."3

---

3 Bartleby. (2022, September 3). Talking it over. *The Economist*, 57.

Finally, the real motivation for developing others requires finding satisfaction in the success of others. When we find joy in seeing others exceed our capacities and go on to greater roles than we have attained, we have found the motivational source of people development. The fact that *we get to do this* is a wonderful part of our leadership careers.

Now that you've had a chance to think about it, which of these motives resonates with you?

What will you do differently to develop others?

A Personal Story

I had a deeply challenging team member. I was ready to terminate the individual. I thought, *I'm going to give this one last try.* So, we had a conversation. It was intense, direct, and clear. I offered my assistance to help him develop if he was willing to work with me. If he chose to do so, he could stay on the team. Otherwise, he would leave. He got focused and worked with me. Nearly a year later, the individual offered this: "Your feedback has not only changed my work, but my marriage and family life as well." That moment was deeply satisfying.

It's important to understand that leader satisfaction is a corollary outcome in developing people.

With so much focus on employee satisfaction, we've lost sight of a significant factor in organizational effectiveness: leader satisfaction. Without satisfied leaders, employee engagement scores are likely to remain the same as they have for decades. Leaders are continually (and appropriately) held accountable for project success, the achievement of strategic plans, annual budgets, disciplinary actions, corporate compliance, and the day-to-day actions of reporting and execution. But we'd all agree that there's more to life than merely accomplishing tasks. A life's work as a leader can carry a much deeper meaning and impact. That's where the high calling of people development comes in. Leaders can assess their own satisfaction with their work by taking the time to reflect on their personal impact on their employees.

Developing others gives leaders a sense of purpose and value.

As we've discussed, the word *development* can feel like corporate speak—just another box to check. But good leaders *do* develop people. And leaders gain satisfaction from employee development, both short-term and over the long haul. It's a win-win.

Assessing people's skills and taking those to the next level is part of developing people. Assigning developmental tasks will improve the competence of our people. Overall, a significant part of our satisfaction as leaders depends on inspiring others to levels of achievement they never dreamed were possible!

Here are a few statements to assess your satisfaction as a leader.

I *know* my influence has improved the competence of the individuals I have led because....

I sense a great deal of pride when one of the people I've hired goes on to greater things than I have achieved. One person who comes to mind is...

The model of leadership I have demonstrated has changed the lives of others, and here's the proof:

CHAPTER 3 SYNOPSIS

Leaders can find deep satisfaction developing others by taking the long view and discovering that the success of others is the primary reason for doing development work. Leaders can find personal satisfaction in the leadership influence they exert through developing people. Development is a calling we leaders are privileged to do. *We get to do this.*

Let's go on to consider some specific things about the people we develop.

SOME CONSIDERATIONS ABOUT THE PEOPLE WE DEVELOP

WORKING DEFINITION

People Development is the process of

(1) gaining new knowledge,

(2) learning new skills,

(3) improving efficacy,

(4) strengthening existing capabilities, and

(5) gaining achievements that validate someone's value in the organization.

Team members come in all varieties, new and long-term, experienced and inexperienced, cautious and outgoing, introverted and extroverted. The variations are endless, because each person is unique. And great leadership assesses people as they are, not as we would wish them to be. Development is how we invest in them to move them forward.

To highlight this topic, schedule a meeting to exclusively discuss this subject. Even though your employees may desire to gain new experiences, they may not even know about the concept of development. Setting aside time to discuss where they think they'd like to develop opens a context for them to freely talk about the subject as they go about their daily work and as they think about their long-term goals. This is not a time to make promises, it is a time to learn about employee aspirations.

New People

Anytime we bring on a new team member, we meet someone with existing experiences, both good and bad, and those experiences can be useful to our organization. We gain someone who has both strengths and weaknesses, and we gain someone who wants to make a contribution. When considering employee development, we must acknowledge that no one comes to us as a *tabula rasa*, a blank slate. So it's up to us as leaders to create development experiences for newcomers that add value to our organization. The primary reason is that the context of our organization may be different from other organizations they have served in the past.

Long-term Tenured Employees

But it's not just new employees who need development experiences. Long-term employees seek development too, but they have different expectations because of their multiyear relationship with a manager. Long-term employees represent a great challenge because of their knowledge of the organization and because they've been through many development scenarios. Leaders must think deeply about how to increase the capacity of long-term employees. Anything that smacks of trendy, novel, or popular may be met with skepticism. Developing long-term employees requires deep thinking and effort on the part of the leader.

Why Long-term Team Members Present a Special Challenge in Development

Over time and a career, employee development needs change. People who have been with us for a long time have completely different development motivations than those who are new to our company or are fresh out of school. A leader's job becomes more complex the longer we have someone on our team. We've given them projects and tasks, along with useful assignments. They know our approach and methods. But the value of a long-term team member is the relationship we've developed. It gives us the background to find out what they'd like to do and then take action to ensure they get there.

Long-Term Employees Transferred to our Team
– the toughest group

We also face the challenge of gaining long-term team members who have worked for others who may have failed them in the past, perhaps making promises that were not fulfilled. Thus, they carry some cynicism about learning new things. Gaining the confidence of long-term employees takes significant effort. Nonetheless, as leaders, we can find ways to help them develop. Tenure on their part does not mean an excuse on our part.

Technical versus Social Employees

Engineers (and technical team members in general) seek development opportunities that are often different from marketing or salespeople. (Funny thing is, however, they can all learn from each other in the bigger scheme of development). Technical people generally need development in communication and presentation. Social people generally need development in accuracy, analysis, and argument building.

Carrie Lauersdorf, engineer and project manager, explains the interesting challenge for development of tech people. "Leaders select people to fill a seat on the bus. However, as someone on the bus with a technical degree, I don't know where we're going or how to change seats. We usually have a niche, and if we leave, the leader assigns a new body to the seat."

She goes on to say, "You love what you do, but something is taking your joy away. Thinking about these types of technical individuals, I feel if they received development in speaking/presenting and in soft skills, they could soar."

Everyone wants development opportunities.

Fact is, all employees are looking to their managers to bring good development experiences to their lives. Each individual has an interest that sparks motivation for development. There is something everyone seeks to enrich their careers, something that excites them and fuels their internal motivation to improve. So, leaders need to pay attention to the things that activate motivation for development. Just observing people and their work situations can give us insight into where they need development.

For starters, there's a value to simply *listening* to what people are saying they lack in their development.

What do people mention in passing? They give us clues to what they really want to improve.

Where do you see them struggle?

And what intuitions do you have about what they need based on their conversations? (What have trusted colleagues mentioned about your team members?)

ABOUT LIKING PEOPLE

One basic thing leaders must understand: we will not like all of our employees, but that should not play a role in whether we take the time to develop them. Liking people is an instinct, an inexplicable emotional connection. No one really understands why we like someone. Could be a personality that matches ours, could be mutual interests, or it could be a natural connection to the job. It could be lots of things, but it's impossible to know why liking happens. That's important for us to recognize from the get-go, because managing people means considering the entire team, not just the people we like. (One of the major mistakes I made early in my management career was liking people, and it was perceived as favoritism—an unpleasant discovery for me.) Though we may dislike some of our team members, we still have an obligation to develop them.

Let's go a little deeper.

When people ask to be developed, here's what I believe they mean:

1. *They want to learn new things to add to their list of skills (part of our definition).*

   Development means increased knowledge and strengthened ability in a specific domain of learning. There is satisfaction in simply learning new things. Whatever we learn in life, we can take with us. The learning adds to our value and our understanding of others. Who among us has not experienced deep satisfaction by learning something complex?

2. *They want to be challenged but not overwhelmed.*

   Challenging projects develop people, so long as they're not overwhelmed by the challenge. When that happens, their manager has not effectively evaluated an employee's capabilities. This requires some quick rethinking and careful coaching, taking the time to ensure the employee understands the risks and has access to the leader if things go sideways. If someone is overwhelmed by an assignment, they want to know you're there to help if needed.

3. *They want to find satisfaction in their current role.*

   Sometimes people want to enjoy the role they have with *increased depth*. A finance person may be quite comfortable in their chosen role and desire to get *really good* at finance—to be respected as an expert's expert with more certifications and industry-level acknowledgements. Engineers often follow this pattern as well.

4. *They want to be prepared for the next role.*

Some seek opportunities in their current role to prepare them for the next stage of their career. The possibility of promotion is a significant motive in development opportunities. (Managers must be careful not to promise a promotion that may not happen).

5. *They want to add richness to their careers (and parenthetically, their lives).*

Some have become stagnant in their current role and want to add knowledge or experience to reboot a fresh interest in their job. The job has become routine, and they know it well, but that's no longer enough. They want to develop more aspects of their job, whether on the people side or the technical side.

6. *They want to address a gap in their capabilities.*

Some people want to fix a weakness they see in their performance. It may have been an issue brought up in a review, or it may have become evident during a complex project where they (or perhaps someone else) felt they were missing key skills. It may have been a gap pointed out by peers. A carefully chosen development project can overcome a weakness in capabilities.

7. *Ultimately, people get bored when they're not challenged!*

Challenging work makes life more interesting, and people want to do interesting things. Without some development work along the way, people become stale, and those who become stale often start to complain and lose productivity (and negatively impact the team). Sometimes, the hamster wheel can become a drudgery, causing people to lose interest in committing more energy to their team and their company. Boredom takes a toll, and without development, they lose interest in bringing their best.

Now, think about the team members who work for you. Which of these seven development elements do your team members seek?

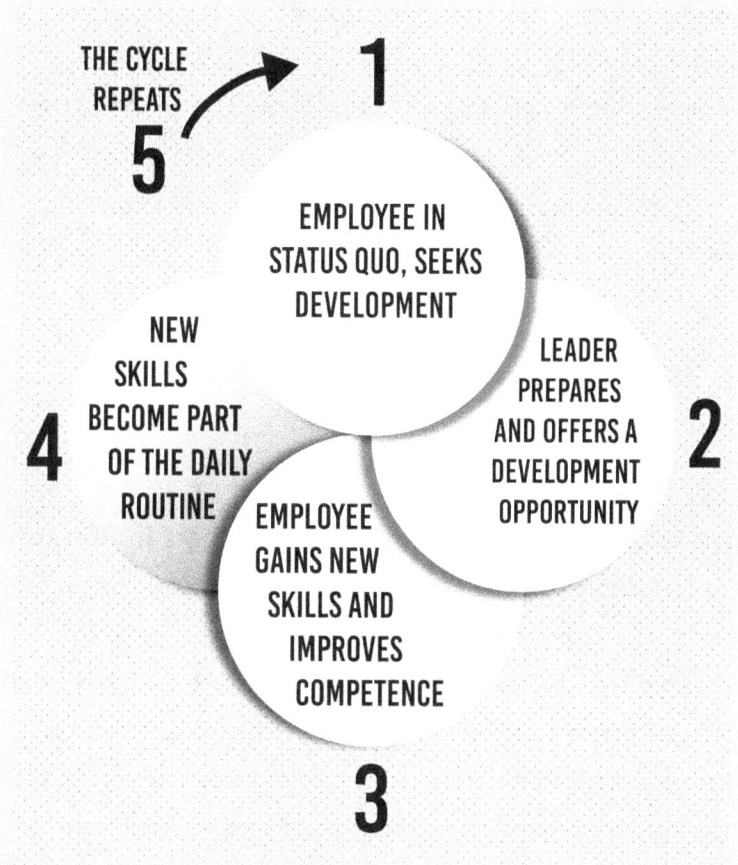

As our tenure with an employee continues, we recognize the cycle of development will—indeed *must*—repeat itself. Once an individual achieves a level of competence in one area, they'll want (and need!) to improve other skills. They may overcome a huge obstacle and gain confidence in the process, and then become bored and need further developmental challenges. This happens because they are developing self-efficacy. The cycle of development repeats.

1. The employee finds herself in status quo and becomes less engaged in role, seeking development.

2. The leader considers and offers a development opportunity.

3. The employee gains new skills and improves competence, benefiting the organization.

4. New skills become part of the daily routine.

5. The cycle repeats itself.

Case Studies: A Managerial Look at the Challenges of Developing Five Different Employees

Consider the differences of developing the following five people. Each of them has different career intentions and goals, thus leaders need to find development projects or learning that guide people to greater levels of performance and achievement.

Jill: New employee, fresh out of college, excited to be part of the organization and looking to you for guidance and development. After she has learned the basics of the organization through onboarding, there are many developmental opportunities for Jill.

Mohir: Successful, dependable, not interested in too much development. Mohir is a steady Eddie, always willing to get the job done, but not much more. Mohir has a lot of room for growth, he has untapped capacity, but he is content to do just enough to get by every day.

Jan: Strong employee with long tenure and skilled in one area. Jan knows his stuff. Few can compete with his skills in engineering. People go to Jan for the answers to deeply complex questions, and he comes through every time. But Jan has mentioned he feels he's getting stale and stagnant in his role and needs a challenge.

Bob: Old-timer who has been with the company forever. Bob is a plodder who wants nothing to do with development. His focus is on weekend fishing.

Anita: Rock star with multiple skills, who feels she wants to manage her own development and is energized to take things into her own hands and move faster than her leader.

The Exercise: Improve Your Skill!

So, we have different employees with completely different goals and needs. Consider what motivation to activate as we continue the development process. What does this person want to develop? Even more important, how can we demonstrate our leadership by assessing what they really need and offer opportunities for them to develop in a new area where they have the capacity but lack important skills? If you had to work with these individuals, what approach would you use to develop each one?

Reread the five employee profiles on the previous pages. Create a people development approach for each employee.

Jill

Mohir

Jan

Bob

Anita

CHAPTER 4 SYNOPSIS

We've looked a bit deeper into different types of people on our teams and the individual needs they bring to the development process. We took a deeper look at why people want development, ranging from overcoming weaknesses to enhancing a specific skill set to future promotion. Each employee has a different reason for development that leaders must attend to when choosing assignment or projects.

It's time to take a deeper look at how elements of motivation influence development.

CREATING THE CONDITIONS FOR MOTIVATION

WORKING DEFINITION

People Development is the process of

(1) gaining new knowledge,

(2) learning new skills,

(3) improving efficacy,

(4) strengthening existing capabilities, and

(5) gaining achievements that validate someone's value in the organization.

Development requires a grasp of motivation theory because we need to understand what really drives people to accomplish something new, including their own development. We often hear that "leaders motivate people." At the risk of organizational heresy, I disagree. *Leaders don't motivate anyone.* But they do create the conditions that activate motivation, which is critical for development. Researchers such as Daniel Pink, Albert Bandura, Deci & Ryan, and Robert White did the hard work of providing insight into the following motivations.

Effectance Motivation: The sense that I'm making a difference and creating successful outcomes

Competence Motivation: The sense that I have the skill and ability to accomplish tasks

Autonomy Motivation: The sense that I am free to influence things that affect my life

Relatedness Motivation: The sense of well-being I attain by being with people I like, and who like me

Efficacy Motivation: The sense I can control an outcome

Here's a question: Does any leader *really* have access to these powerful *internal* motivations? The answer is a profound **no.** The only one who has access is the person—*the motivation belongs to them alone.* The fusion reactors of internal motivation are at the disposal of the one who owns the reactor.

Yes, people can be *forced* to be comply, to make a difference, but their performance will be weaker than when they freely choose. Motivation is powerful, but also very delicate. "Commitment is always better than compliance," wrote Mike Markiewicz.

We cannot expect to simply draw motivation out of people as if they have a switch leaders can turn on and off. There is no certain cause and effect. Leaders understand that no amount of speaking, PowerPoints, or morale-boosting posters will create motivation. They know they must *create the conditions to activate natural human motivation.*

So, let's take a look at some motivations common to all people.

Leaders create the conditions to activate natural human motivation through careful, thoughtful, intentional, and deliberate actions. *The purpose for understanding these motivations is to tap them in development.* We don't always need a personality profile or psychological instrument. Sometimes our instincts and observations is all we need to sort out the driving motivation of our employees.

Let's start with some basic, day-to-day activities that demonstrate these five motivations. Then we'll look carefully at how to activate them in development.

The Five Basic Motivations in the Context of Development

Effectance Motivation: *The sense that I am making a difference and creating outcomes*

People often say, "I want to make a difference." This is effectance motivation. In the context of development, effectance motivation is activated when someone is part of something greater than themselves. An example of this is working on something that has an impact within your organization. In a development context, leaders can present new projects as opportunities for employees to have a dramatic impact on their companies. This could include things like lunch and learns or offering them an opportunity to present to their team.

Thinking about your team, which of your team members has a desire for effectance?

Competence Motivation: *The sense that I have the skill and ability to accomplish tasks*

All people want to be competent, but some want to achieve an extremely high level of competence to fulfill a need for self-worth. In a development context, this means a manager assigns an employee an opportunity to increase competence in a particular domain—could be attending a workshop, offering an opportunity to work with other experts, or demonstrating their capability outside a company presenting new concepts and ideas.

COMPETENCE MOTIVATION

Thinking about your team, which of your team members has a desire for competence?

Autonomy Motivation: *The sense that I am free to influence things that affect my life*

People want to have a major influence on their career development because the time they spend in their organizations impacts their lives. In a development context, managers can provide ways for employees to steer their careers, to select development opportunities from a range of choices, and to state which projects *they* would like to be involved in.

AUTONOMY MOTIVATION

Thinking about your team, which of your team members has a desire for autonomy?

Relatedness Motivation: *The sense of well-being I attain by being with people I like, and who like me*

People who tend to be more social want to spend time with others during their development. This is sometimes called affiliation, a craving to belong and contribute. Managers can create true team events in which employees gain an opportunity to build relationships with others in their group. This is generally done in social settings, but it can be a strong development opportunity for someone who seeks relatedness.

Community or volunteer activities also fall into this category, for example, leading a community action with high schools or nonprofits.

RELATEDNESS MOTIVATION

Thinking about your team, which of your team members has a desire for relatedness?

Efficacy Motivation: *The sense that I can control an outcome*

Part of career growth is a personal sense of improved efficacy—confidence—in the ability to manage demanding or difficult situations. In a development context, leaders offer difficult projects, but coach their team members through them, offering support as the project continues.

Thinking about your team, which of your team members has a desire for increased efficacy?

EFFICACY MOTIVATION

Thinking about your team, which of your team members has a desire for increased efficacy?

Specific Behaviors You Can Choose to Activate Motivation

As a leader, you have options to activate human motivation. I am listing several behaviors under each motivation, so you can select the ones that will increase a specific motivation for an individual.

Effectance Motivation: *I am making a difference.*

Daily behaviors that activate effectance motivation:

1. Consistently provide timely feedback on employee results.

2. Communicate the purpose and goals of employee roles.

3. Share data with employees to show them how they're doing, including customer feedback.

4. Provide legitimate rewards for a job well done.

5. Let employees critique the process.

6. Give them an opportunity to share in planning processes.

7. Acknowledge best practices.

8. Take the time to help them find an emotional connection to what they do.

Competence Motivation: *I am good at what I do.*

Daily behaviors that activate competence motivation:

1. Plan to address several learning styles—verbal, visual, kinesthetic, social, observational.

2. Train to specific needs in projects.

3. Mentor and share your knowledge.

4. Clarify that there are no stupid questions. Learning trumps winning.

5. Implement job rotations that make sense.

6. Ensure understanding of new information by doing a quick follow-up after learning.

7. Provide clarity of organizational structures.

8. Share metrics that demonstrate improvement.

Autonomy Motivation: *I have freedom to influence.*

Daily behaviors that influence autonomy motivation:

1. Demonstrate trust—don't micromanage.

2. Be cautious about how you manage failure. Short of something unethical, failure is not pleasant for anyone, but if we want to maintain team morale, we need to discuss the failure and reasons for it to ensure learning.

3. Ask, then listen.

4. Provide guidelines, then get out of the way.

5. Provide structure in decision-making, but leave the details to team members.

6. Be flexible.

7. Keep team members involved in the process.

8. Provide active communication that helps people make good decisions.

Relatedness Motivation: *I like these people and they like me.*

Daily behaviors that activate relatedness motivation:

1. Share success as a team.

2. Share best practices.

3. Plan social outings. (I once had a team outing teaching baseball to a group of IT engineers from India. What fun it was watching the cricket players attempt to learn American baseball! We had a blast, and we bonded.)

4. Use the entire team on big projects.

5. Make room for people to laugh.

6. Work with other leaders to create cross-departmental engagement.

7. Conduct one-on-ones with the leader to develop a professional rapport.

Efficacy motivation: *I can control an outcome.*

Daily behaviors that activate efficacy motivation:

1. Assign projects that stretch a person without overwhelming them.

2. Recognize people when they have accomplished something big, and remind them that what once seemed overwhelming is now part of their repertoire of achievement.

3. Coach people through a project to ensure they succeed.

**So, here are our five employees,
and the motivational resources to tap**

Effectance Motivation: The sense that I'm making a difference and creating successful outcomes

Competence Motivation: The sense that I have the skill and ability to accomplish tasks

Autonomy Motivation: The sense that I am free to influence things that affect my life

Relatedness Motivation: The sense of well-being I attain by being with people I like, and who like me

Efficacy Motivation: The sense I can control an outcome

Person	Strengths	Needs to Improve (development)	Challenges	Motivational Resource
Jill	High level of energy	Desire to learn the organization	Where to start	Competence
Mohir	Experience	Step out of routine	Picking the right project	Effectance
Jan	Deep knowledge	Extend his knowledge across the organization	Convincing Jan to try something new	Autonomy
Bob	Reliable	Bring more to the table	Getting Bob engaged without causing trouble	Efficacy
Anita	Expertise, capacity for work	Patience with others, guiding those who don't report to her	Taking on too much at one time	Relatedness

CHAPTER 5 SYNOPSIS

Motivation is, arguably, a big subject, but it's important for us to consider when thoughtfully developing our people. We reviewed five big motivations common to all people, and then discovered detailed actions to take when developing people around those motivations. We evaluated some individuals to discover how to activate motivation in their work lives.

Now let's take a look at some specific ways to develop people, including shallow water and deep-water development.

SHALLOW WATER OR DEEP WATER?

People Development is the process of

(1) gaining new knowledge,

(2) learning new skills,

(3) improving efficacy,

(4) strengthening existing capabilities, and

(5) gaining achievements that validate someone's value in the organization.

When we think about developing people, it's good to have a starting point of actions and ideas, a list of specific ways employees can be developed. I believe leaders are sometimes at a loss; they don't know what development opportunities they should offer their team members. So, here's a list of ideas and concepts for you to consider with each of your team members! (Sometimes just having a starting point gives us better ideas—that's my intention for you in this section).

Each of the following activities and projects strengthens the team member, ultimately increasing the effectiveness of the team and the organization.

Opportunities for employee development are broadly divided into two major categories: *skills*-focused development (tends to be individual activities) and *people*-focused development (engaging a wider group of team members).

SKILLS-FOCUSED DEVELOPMENT

Each of the following skills are transferable. The employee takes the skill with them wherever they go. (This is a good reminder for your team members. The new skills they develop become part of their repertoire.)

Communication. Effective written and verbal interactions are the lifeblood of a group. How well does your employee communicate with others? Consider different levels of the organization—staff, line level, mid-level, and senior leadership.

Presentation skills. Gaining audience attention and persuading through facts is an essential skill. How well does your employee present to others?

Technical capacities. There are several software tools that enhance skill levels, including Excel, Project Management, and others. Managers could offer workshops for high-end technical skills.

Accountability. This is how to ensure things get finished. Is your employee effective at getting things done?

Poise and professionalism. These qualities shine through as a personal brand of excellence. Does your team member need help understanding how they come across to others?

Executive condensing. Can they get to the point...quickly? This skill is not as easy as it sounds. One of my friends said this of the classic elevator pitch: "His elevator pitch is so long he'll need a sky-scraper." This is a critical skill for career development. Executive condensing is finding the heart of a communication point, making it clearly (within seconds) and with confidence, conveying an impression of competence.

Politics. How well does your team member navigate the complexity of conflicting interests within the company? How do they assess which decision maker is most critical to the success of a project?

Specific areas of development around primary expertise: Finance, Legal, HR, and operational skills fall into this category.

Now, prioritize these skills for your team members.
Considering each of your team members, which of these skills is the highest priority for their development today?

Skill	Team Member who needs Development
Communication	
Presentation skills	
Technical capacities	
Accountability	
Poise and professionalism	
Executive condensing	
Specific areas of development around their primary expertise	

Conflict management: How well does your team member resolve difficult and stressful situations in the workplace?

Collaboration: Does your team member have the ability to effectively work with peers and other departments without a reporting relationship?

Recognition: Does your employee have the insight and skill to *effectively* reward others?

Managing Change: How well does your team member introduce and manage change all the way to completion?

Coalition building: Can your team member effectively bring people together to accomplish something greater?

Leading teams: How well does your team member organize people to accomplish complex projects?

Politics: How well does your team member navigate the complexity of differing and conflicting interests within the company? How do they assess which decision maker is most critical to the success of a project?

Leading meetings effectively: A meeting can be a disaster or a great experience, and it all depends on the skills of the leader.

Considering each of your team members, which of these skills is the highest priority for their development today?

Skill	Team Member who needs Development
Conflict management	
Collaboration	
Recognition	
Managing change	
Coalition building	
Leading teams	
Politics	
Leading meetings	

Now that we've listed a number of development options, let's take a step further and look at a different way to categorize development. Leaders must make deliberate choices about what developmental actions to take when working with employees. A simple way to look at this is shallow water and deep water. Let me explain.

When we're learning to swim, shallow water presents something new without danger. We can wade into shallow water without getting into trouble. But when we truly learn to swim, we get into deep water where there is no bottom and we're on our own with our own energy and judgment to get us through the situation.

The same thing is true of development. Shallow water presents less risk, while deep water is an intense risk for you as a leader, for the employee, and for the company. The judgment call of development comes down to you as a leader. Have you assessed which employees are ready for deep water development?

Shallow water allows people to learn new things without much danger to the company, to you as a leader, or to the employee.

Shallow water development includes:

* Reading a book and having a discussion with the team or leader

* Training classes: the list is endless (!)

* Mentoring: finding someone to work one-on-one with an employee

* Addressing process issues: what can be done to improve a process?

* Special projects: taking on an issue or challenge that requires investigation

* Job shadowing

* Leading/participating in lunch and learn sessions

* Joining an industry or professional organization (e.g., International Coach Association, Strategic Capability Network), serving on a Board of Directors

* Cross training

* Leader coaching or peer group coaching

* Internal or external coaching

Pushing people into deep water is risky—for you, for them, for the organization. If the project fails, there is a great impact for all involved: their reputation, your reputation, or organizational losses. If you give your team member an opportunity to lead a complex project, what outcomes do you expect? If you give them an opportunity to solve a chronic organizational problem, what outcomes do you expect? You need to make those expectations clear and let them know you'll be supporting them along the way.

Deep water development includes:

Mergers and acquisitions. The deep experience of understanding the intricacies of bringing one company under the umbrella of another is a dramatic development experience. This activity often includes work with high-level executives under significant stress.

Reorganization. Participating in the complex issues of changing company roles is a tough development challenge for the right person.

Cross-functional teams with organizational impact:

1. adding new I.T. systems,

2. engaging in new employee benefits packages,

3. customer input sessions, and

4. relocation teams are examples of deep-water projects to develop the right team member.

There is immense development value when an employee takes on a leadership role in a complex project, including influence, project planning, capacity assessment, and increased foresight/ risk management. It is the art of leadership to know when an employee is ready for this kind of role on top of their current workload. The benefits of a successful "deep water" project cannot be overstated. Many of these projects are career accelerating and will dramatically change a person's visibility in the organization and in the trajectory of their career.

The leader's role is to ensure a person is ready for the deep water.

Follow-up! Follow-up! Follow-up!

Important! No matter what development project you assign your team member, follow-up is essential.

1. Follow up with a frequent check-in: "How's the project going?"

2. Follow up with consistent offers of support.

3. Follow up with planned milestones that can be useful in performance reviews.

4. Ensuring follow-up demonstrates your interest in these team members—and they'll thank you for it!

Summary

In complex, deep-water development experiences, employees engage more than one motivation. Competence, autonomy, relatedness, efficacy, and effectance are all activated (and built!) in complex scenarios. Given the number of development categories and facets available to leaders, there is every reason to spend time and focused effort engaging team members in development activities.

CHAPTER 6 SYNOPSIS

We've looked at a long list of potential development activities and categorized them as more or less complex, individual-based, or team-based. Shallow water is for less experienced team members, while deep water is for those with the capacity to manage large and more complex situations.

Let's take a look at specific team member development.

THE DEVELOPMENT ZONE

Everyone has a role; everyone has a responsibility.

WORKING DEFINITION

People Development is the process of

(1) gaining new knowledge,

(2) learning new skills,

(3) improving efficacy,

(4) strengthening existing capabilities, and

(5) gaining achievements that validate someone's value in the organization.

N ow we're focused exclusively on one person, one individual with whom we work every day. This is the person we're going to develop, both short- and long-term. What will it take one-on-one?

Before we get into the relationship with an employee, every leader must first take time to reflect on their own strengths and weakness in developing people.

Leader Self-Evaluation

To effectively develop people, a leader must fully understand how *they* interact with others. How do you like to communicate? How well do you listen? How well do you follow through? Are you introverted or extroverted, and what difference does that make when you evaluate how to develop an employee?

The answers to each of these questions makes us wiser when we enter the development zone.

As leaders, we need to know ourselves and first consider our own strengths and weaknesses, then use that knowledge effectively when mentoring our team members. By knowing ourselves, we stand a better chance of developing others.

Ponder these questions in the context of working directly with an employee, face-to-face, in a development situation.

When considering how I develop people, my greatest strengths as a leader are:

When considering how I develop people, my weaknesses include:

Changing the lens just a bit, here are two questions to activate motivation for both employees and leaders.

Two questions for employees to consider when seeking development opportunities

1. How can I become the best employee this manager or company has ever seen?

2. How can I be legendary?

The driving motivation of self-respect inspires excellence. When employees challenge themselves to be their best, they increase their capacity, learn new things, improve people skills, and advance their careers.

TWO QUESTIONS FOR MANAGERS

Two questions for managers to ask themselves.

1. How can I help this employee to become the best this company has ever seen?

2. How can they be legendary?

Yes, leaders can ask these questions! The answers may surprise you!

The Heart of the Development Process

At the heart of the development process for the individual employee, there are two critical starting points: *relationship* and *trust*.

A. **Day-to-day Relationship**: The beginning of all management is a basic, personal assessment of your relationship with an employee. Consider the fundamentals—just the basics. Do you know the person reasonably well? Their work habits, schedule, some light interests? Have you had the occasional conversation with them at lunch to simply develop a comfortable space for conversation? Do you know the employee's preferred method of communication?

As mentioned above, we may like some employees more than others, but building a relationship with *all* team members is critical for developmental success. Relationship gives us insight into what people need.

"One point for your consideration: Leaders need to take the time to know their people, so they can determine their development needs, but also to know their strengths, weaknesses, likes, dislikes, who they work best with, etc. The logic in knowing this information is that it informs the leader of where they are the best fit on a project team, or when given a specific task. You don't want to assign someone who is having personal struggles at home to your organization's most important project. When we know our people, we know what they can best help us to achieve."

— Monte Pedersen

B. **Trust between leader and team member**: The key element of trust is essential prior to enlisting a team member in a development project. As you think about your own style and relationship with your team members, have you developed a basic level of trust in your style, in your actions and behaviors, that encourages them to accept your development recommendations? Have you followed through on promises? Have you had their back when things got tough? Have you given them good feedback throughout the year, not just during review time?

Manager and Employee Responsibilities in Development

Development is the process of learning new skills, improving efficacy, strengthening existing capabilities, and gaining achievements that validate someone's value in the organization.

A. **Manager Responsibility:** Managers bear the heavier responsibility for development. Here are some considerations.

  1. As someone responsible for managing the resources of the corporation, we need to consider individual, team, and organizational needs.

  2. As managers, we first need to explain our interest in the development process—not overpromising but offering an understanding that we can work with employees who want to develop.

3. We need to make it clear that we cannot read minds, and so we need to enlist the employee in the development process. A candid discussion about what employees are looking for is a good way to get the process started.

4. Leaders need to discuss the value of development goals for employees, focusing on employee success.

5. Take the time to explain the value of the employee development to the success of the organization.

6. It is *critical* that organizational support is thoughtfully built into any development activity. The essential element of support is one's superior. Ensuring one's boss has insight into the development prospect is always a good idea.

7. The leader may set the expectation that the employee shares their learnings within the organization.

8. Knowing the workload of the employee is 101. We can't just add things to people's plates without ensuring they're able to carry the load.

9. Follow up!

"Too often, people are given development opportunities (purchasing online learning catalogs, for example), but the organization doesn't reduce workload or make time to develop. People are forced to find time on their own, and most people don't get around to it."
— Mike Markiewicz

B. Employee Responsibility. While managers and leaders clearly have a big responsibility in the development of their teams, an overlooked component of development is the employee's responsibility.

1. Ultimately, employees should consider: "How do I enhance my expertise?" And enhancing one's expertise means taking the time to add development to their work activities.

2. Employees have the responsibility to prepare for development conversations with their leader with ideas of how and in what areas they would like to grow and develop.

3. Employees have the responsibility to discuss their development interests with their manager. Is there a specific area in which they'd like to develop?

4. Is there a position in the organization they aspire to?

5. Employees have the responsibility to follow through on the development opportunity to gain from the time spent in the development experience.

6. Most important: Employees have the responsibility to bring something back to the organization.

What comes to mind when you assess your team members? As mentioned above, some elements of development cost money. Workshops are pricey and may include travel expenses.

Skills-Based Assessments

Communication. Effective written and verbal interactions are the group's lifeblood. How well does your employee communicate with others? Consider different levels of the organization—staff, line level, mid-level, and senior leadership.

Presentation skills. Gaining audience attention and persuading through facts is an essential skill. How well does your employee present to others?

Technical capacities. There are several software tools that enhance skill levels, including Excel, Project Management, and others. Managers could offer workshops for high-end technical skills.

Accountability. This is how to ensure things get finished. Is your employee effective at getting things done?

Poise and Professionalism. These qualities shine through as a personal brand of excellence. Does your team member need help understanding how they come across?

Executive condensing. Can they get to the point...quickly? This skill is not as easy as it sounds. One of my friends said this of the classic elevator pitch: "His elevator pitch is so long he'll need a skyscraper." This is a critical skill for career development. Executive condensing is finding the heart of a communication point, making it clearly (within seconds) and with confidence, conveying an impression of competence.

Specific areas of development around primary expertise*:* Finance, legal, HR, and operational skills fall into this category.

People-Based Assessments

Conflict management. How well does your team member resolve difficult and stressful situations in the workplace?

Collaboration. Is your team member able to effectively work with peers and other departments without a reporting relationship?

Recognition. Does your employee have the insight and skill to *effectively* reward others?

Managing change. How well does your team member introduce and manage change all the way to completion?

Coalition building. Can your team member effectively bring people together to accomplish something greater?

Leading teams. How well does your team member organize people to accomplish complex projects?

Politics. How well does your team member navigate the complexity of conflicting interests within the company? How do they assess which decision maker is most critical to the success of a project?

Leading meetings effectively. A meeting can be a disaster or a great experience, and it all depends on the skills of the leader.

1. How do we invest thousands of dollars in the best way possible? What project is going to expand their skill set?

2. What activity will bring them greater influence in the company?

3. What personal satisfaction will the team member derive from the experience?

4. How will *they* change because of the development task, action, or project?

5. And how will their improved skillset benefit the organization?

Managerial judgment weighs organizational strategies and goals against individual employee needs.

What _organizational_ goal do we accomplish as we develop this individual employee?

That's important because it lays the groundwork, explaining the why to an employee. For example, "Here's the value to the organization, and here's the value to you." By informing the team member how their efforts in a development activity benefit the organization, you connect them to the meaningful power of organizational success. They're part of something bigger than themselves.

A manager must not neglect to explain how a person positively impacts their organization. People spend years working and sometimes have no clue how they have benefited the organization. It's a good thing to remind them. _People like to know they matter._ Informing them of their value to the organization is a meaningful way to explain a development opportunity. The more specific we can be, the better. "Here's where your work on project XYZ is impacting company strategy ABC."

The balance between organizational and individual needs is highlighted below. It's never either/or; it's always both/and. The individual benefits and grows, while the organization gets stronger. It's essential that a leader understands how developing one person can have a major impact on a team, a division, and the entire organization.

Balancing Organizational and Individual Goals

Organizational Goals and Strategies

Organizational Benefits

Employee Development Needs

Internal Employee Motivation

SPECIFIC SKILL ANALYSIS

A systematic way of developing a range of options for developing communication skills is to lay out a simple decision grid. It always helps to see options on a piece of paper (or a screen) because the brain can only handle so much is our decision-making process. Our first example is something nearly every team member can benefit from—improving communication. Let's look at some options.

Example 1: Developing a range of options for developing communication skills

Developing Communication Skills

Need for development	Development Option	Pro	Con
Communication	Workshop	In depth, thorough, offsite, focused	Expense and time away; may not include practice
Communication	One-to-one mentoring	Timely	Requires the right mentor
Communication	Role model of outstanding practice	Observation of excellence in a role	Takes effort from manager to find the right person
Communication	One-on-one coaching with an internal or external presentation skills or communication coach	Internal coaches have knowledge of communication messages and culture of the company	Internal coaches may be biased or not as highly skilled as external coaches

By simply laying out these options on paper, a leader can gain insight into which project, task, or approach to use in development, with the long-term benefit of having a plan in a file for future development ideas.

Example 2: Analyzing a range of options for developing influence skills

Another area that just about any employee can improve is influence. Influence has impact across organizations, so the stronger your team becomes, the more they can impact organizational decisions about funding, data, hiring choices, and more.

Developing Influence Skills

Need for development	Development Option	Pro	Con
Influence	Workshop	In-depth, thorough, offsite, focused	Expense and time away
Influence	Cognitive apprenticeship	Timely	Requires the right mentor
Influence	Role model of outstanding practice	Observation of excellence in a role	Takes effort from manager to find the right person

Let's consider some scenarios from the people we've met along the way.

#1 Jenson Corporation is going through a major reorganization and needs a team leader to build communications for the project. **Jill** is a capable leader who has good communication skills but could benefit from working on a major project.

#2 Rodeo Corporate is rolling out a new benefits program and needs a team leader to keep all the moving parts on track. The project has high corporate visibility. **Mohir** has been seeking ways to improve his corporate visibility.

#3 Chronos Company is developing new 3D-modeling processes and needs increased technical capability. **Jan** has an engineering degree but needs additional training to be successful in a subject matter role.

#4 Capital Holdings is seeking an outside consultant to manage a new change. **Anita** has a Change Management background from another company and could do well while gaining critical corporate visibility.

#5 Guadalupe Enterprises is changing all its corporate signage. **Bob** is an old-timer who could benefit from a fresh look at the company, along with the added value of sharing his concerns about change, since long-term employees are often reluctant to move forward with new ideas.

Each of these scenarios balances the organizational need with the employee need.

What are the big organizational challenges facing your organization right now?

Which of your team members is best suited to help the organization solve that problem?

CHAPTER 7 SYNOPSIS

A leader needs to assess which investment will likely bring about the intended development. This rubric is intended to give leaders a framework for considering where, when, and how much to invest in an employee. We started with the basics of relationship and trust, then considered how the development activity will benefit the organization.

Next stop: Development, while critical, isn't always easy. There can be barriers along the road!

CHAPTER 8

OVERCOMING HINDRANCES TO EMPLOYEE DEVELOPMENT

WORKING DEFINITION:

People Development is the process of

(1) gaining new knowledge,

(2) learning new skills,

(3) improving efficacy,

(4) strengthening existing capabilities, and

(5) gaining achievements that validate someone's value in the organization.

From a Linked In poll July 2022

In your opinion, which of these issues is the primary reason for a lack of employee development?	
You can see how people vote. Learn more	
Manager disinterest.	21%
Employees don't see value.	21%
Lack organizational support.	57%
Manager workload.	0%

Development isn't always easy. There are multiple obstacles that involve the employee, the leader, and the organization. Sometimes things get in the way, and it's important to consider why we're facing a barrier, then adjust our strategy to accomplish the goal of development. It's just good management.

I recall a situation in a restaurant where the waitstaff said to me, "I didn't sign up for this" as she walked away frustrated on a busy Sunday morning because she had too much to do. Sometimes employees have workload issues that cause avoidance of development. Sometimes managers have personal issues that get in the way of development, and sometimes the organization is the problem, not providing enough support for development activities.

Let's take a look at each obstacle.

Obstacles Based in the Person

1. I don't really want to do this. I wasn't hired to do these activities.

2. I'm not really interested in adding extra work to my schedule.

3. I don't have time. I'm really busy.

4. This takes me away from my primary job.

5. I have too much to do.

Thinking about your team, which of these hindrances come to mind?

Typically, resistance shows up as general "folded arms" response. Explaining the organizational need for the development activity establishes a reason for the work. In other words, it isn't optional, but it is beneficial to the company. Another strategy is to explain that other members of the team don't qualify for the particular activity.

The one thing managers can do to alleviate most of these obstacles is to remove a project from the employee and give it to another team member. That way it gets tougher for team members to complain about more work, e.g., development, if their bandwidth has been increased by their manager.

Obstacles Based in the Manager/Leader

1. I am jealous of a talented individual.

2. I fear losing people.

3. I have no time for follow-through.

4. I am too busy to engage employees with work I consider non-essential. If you ask me, development is just fluff.

5. I could lose this person down the road if I invest too much, they'll become too valuable and want to leave.

6. I have no budget and am unwilling to go to bat for the funds.

7. I don't want to spend extra time communicating with the person the way they want to be communicated with.

Thinking about yourself, which of these obstacles come to mind?

Clearly, you must identify *your own reasons for not developing people*, but not investing in people can result in less productivity and increase the risk of losing a great employee. Every employee has a sixth sense about their manager. When employees assess that you're not truly interested in their success and discover a low level of motivation of your part, they'll choose to look elsewhere. It happens all the time. The research overwhelmingly shows that supervisors and managers are the primary reason people leave. Lack of development is at the top of the list.

Organizationally, a leader must put all the pieces into place to ensure a development activity will happen. Making promises that cannot be delivered is a rookie mistake that can erode trust in an employee.

As for losing people, there really is no guarantee someone won't walk even after we've done everything we needed to do. The goal, of course, is to retain the employee, and overall, an 80% retention rate of employees has all the advantages for the organization we've discussed above. Not doing anything is far worse. So, although a leader may fear developing someone may cause them to move on, it's far better to develop someone with the likelihood they'll stay within the organization and tell others about your skills developing people, making you a leader other people want to work for. In other words, your reputation in the organization is built by the way you develop people.

Managing jealousy and other personal issues is up to you. Remember people can detect if something is holding you back from developing them. That feeling can backfire, and ultimately, they'll hold something back from you.

Obstacles Based in the Organization

1. There's not enough surrounding leadership support new development (especially the local leader of a team or department).

2. The manager succeeds in getting people excited to do something different, but they are stifled by organizational politics or managerial restraint.

3. There is a lack of organizational support for the new behavior or knowledge—training and development's nightmare.

4. There are insufficient resources for bigger development experiences like workshops or off-site training.

Each of these obstacles requires managerial expertise to overcome, including overcoming one's own barriers.

Thinking about your organization, which of these obstacles come to mind? And what will *YOU* do to overcome them?

"In my career, I've run ahead of the overall organization when it comes to structural support and organizational tools for employee development. And it's worked, and often the organization catches up with me. My point is that many may use the excuse that the organization doesn't support people development. My responses would be (a) so what, and (b) the organization will fully support the results you achieve through developing your people."

—Barry Keller

Although these obstacles exist, as leaders, we don't have the excuse of saying, "Well, this is too hard. I'll just go back to what I've always done—filling out an employee development plan at the beginning of the year and letting it collect dust." Recall the reasons we develop people: employee satisfaction, retention, and organizational performance. Overcoming barriers isn't just a good idea—it's essential to accomplishing the goals of retaining great employees.

CHAPTER 8 SYNOPSIS

Though it is essential for organizational success, employee development is not always easy. We evaluated obstacles based in the employee, the manager, and the organization. The barriers exist, but good leaders overcome them.

It's time to take a look at a rarely spoken of but important element of managerial behavior that makes all the difference during development: leadership patience.

CHAPTER 9

THE POWER OF LEADERSHIP PATIENCE IN DEVELOPING OTHERS

People Development is the process of

(1) gaining new knowledge,

(2) learning new skills,

(3) improving efficacy,

(4) strengthening existing capabilities, and

(5) gaining achievements that validate someone's value in the organization.

Development requires significant efforts from leaders, not the least of which is patience. Yet organizational pressures compel us to act.

Leaders are under immense organizational pressure to:

1. achieve more revenue and profit than the previous year at a lower less cost and at a faster rate;

2. respond more quickly to customer requests;

3. meet corporate objectives for employee engagement scores;

4. achieve higher levels of customer satisfaction;

5. produce five nines of up-time;

6. meet government requirements;

7. expand into new markets in new geographic territories;

8. and achieve these things ethically, under the scrutiny of the public eye.

This is the reality for today's leaders. And you want me to be...patient?

The answer is <u>yes</u>, especially during the critical actions of development. Leader impatience creates an unwelcome environment for followers, especially during the development process. In times of development, people are more vulnerable to failure, and thus an impatient leader can add more stress to the job. During development, people are at risk of failure. Many who read this have been the object of leadership impatience during a time of development. We know what that's like. It is an unpleasant and unwelcome emotional experience, often leading to discouragement. We've also been impatient with our own followers, and we've seen their reactions.

The Value of Leadership Patience in Development

What's the value of patience in developing others? By exercising patience, we build deeper trust with our team members because they know, beyond the shadow of a doubt, that we are attentive to their concerns during a time of uncertainty. Most likely, we will get better solutions from team members, simply because they will not fear criticism, reprisal, or belittlement.

People learning new things require patience.

1. Consider how incompetent you are when you learn a new software system.

2. Consider how ineffective you feel when you join a new organization or team.

3. Consider how lost you feel when you step into a brand-new team situation.

4. Consider how clumsy you feel conversing with someone in a language you can't speak.

5. Consider how awkward you feel when you think you're on a new team and you find out the idea you suggested was a dismal failure.

All this and more happens when someone is learning something new. And that takes patience on the part of the leader.

Make no mistake: Leader patience *does not equal procrastination*. Procrastination is indecisiveness. Patience is a more complex and powerful leadership attribute. Procrastination drags out decisions; patience leads to more effective decisions. Procrastination makes team members crazy; patience builds their confidence, especially during development.

Leadership patience builds confidence in followers. For the past decades, Daniel Goleman has taught us about the critical impact of leadership emotions in the workplace. We *know* both intuitively and objectively that impatience builds mistrust, fear, anger, resentment, and frustration with our team members. The reverse is also true. Followers who recognize the immense pressures you face as a leader also acknowledge the price of patience. Through patience, leaders find ways to reduce anxiety so people can make effective decisions using their cerebral cortex, instead of the deep emotional centers of the brain.

Leadership patience is the ability to value the personal relationship required to accomplish a goal. Reminder: We tend to overestimate our own abilities!

The two elements of leadership patience are listening and coaching.

1. **Listening.** We've all heard this before, but maybe we weren't listening. Listening is essential during development because the development action is new territory for the team member. The day-to-day stuff rarely requires intensive listening, but during development, listening needs to go up a notch or two. The benefit to the leader is hearing what's really happening during development; the benefit to the team member is reassurance that the leader is paying attention to something that may not be going right. This should be intense listening to ensure things are on the right track. **Rate your listening skills from 1 to 10 with 10 being excellent and 1 being poor.**

2. **Careful Coaching.** It's easy to spout off a few quick ideas to get an employee off your back when you're trying to get something else done (a hundred emails staring you in the face on your computer), but development requires more intentional action. We may need to spend an extra half hour to ensure a development activity is on track. This is deliberate action and effort, asking questions and ensuring comprehension. Set aside the necessary time—and focus. Rate your careful coaching from 1 to 10 with 10 being excellent and 1 being poor.

What to Do When Things Go Wrong

Patience is not easy to learn or practice—especially during employee failure, but it is critical for success when developing people. Yet there is no doubt in my mind that patience impacts our leadership effectiveness. *Here are a few things that worked for me:*

1. **Take a breath** (and maybe a walk down the hall to regroup; maybe splash some water in your face).

2. **Reframe the conversation.** Shy away from failure, and have the employee explain what went wrong. I had a boss model this for me long ago, when I came back from a trip to conduct some research on vibration analysis for installing batteries on vehicles. It went terribly wrong. In fact, it was a disaster. He saw my concern—my hands were literally shaking—and he simply asked what I learned without judgment and offered the next step in the process.

3. Do whatever is necessary to ensure your frustration doesn't degrade the relationship.

Development sometimes goes off track, and things go wrong. We live in an impatient world. While leadership patience is emotionally expensive, leadership impatience is far more costly, especially when employees have moved into the risk-taking of development. We want to be legendary for the right things.

Patience doesn't come naturally to *any* of us. It takes work, but once developed, it provides a deeper foundation for further development of relationship.

CHAPTER 1 SYNOPSIS

Leadership patience is not often spoken about in leadership literature, but patience is essential during development, because new things don't always go as planned for the employee. Leadership patience is essential to maintain and strengthen the relationship between leader and follower during development.

Let's switch to something called cognitive apprenticeship—teaching people how we think about things.

THINKING ABOUT HOW WE THINK

Using Cognitive Apprenticeship to Guide our Teams

WORKING DEFINITION:

People Development is the process of

(1) gaining new knowledge,

(2) learning new skills,

(3) improving efficacy,

(4) strengthening existing capabilities, and

(5) gaining achievements that validate someone's value in the organization.

One of the best things we can do when developing employees is to give them insight into our rules of thumb for navigating the organization. The term *cognitive apprenticeship*[4] was developed a while ago, and it didn't get much traction in the corporate world. But the concept is *ideal* for development. Cognitive

---

4 Journal of Educational Computing, Design & Online learning Volume 4, Fall, 2003 Cognitive Apprenticeship, Technology, and the Contextualization of Learning Environments 1 Cognitive Apprenticeship, Technology, and the Contextualization of Learning Environments Aziz Ghefaili

apprenticeship is simply *explaining*, on the job, how we think about what we do. We're using cognitive skills—*thinking*—to explain how we solve problems. Sharing that insight as part of development goes a long way toward building trust with our team members. Insight into how someone thinks is a gift. Whenever someone can gain a shortcut that saves them time, they're always interested.

Cognitive apprenticeship offers employees a way to navigate the cacophony that occurs in organizations, and there's a lot of it! This typically takes place during the initial stages of development. Taking the time to explain how you think about managing organizational noise is valuable, and many team members consider those insights to be some of the best development actions their leaders can take.

Every day, team members will be faced with myriad inputs, ideas, suggestions, recommendations, prophets of doom, new concepts, sarcastic looks, cynical emails, executive pressure to conform, and a barrage of endless advice.

Explaining how we think is an invaluable development experience for our team members. These discussions open all kinds of interesting doors and stimulate thinking on both sides, creating an intellectual bond between leader and follower.

As we spend time in cognitive apprenticeship, here are some specific areas to discuss.

1. **Teach team members a way to think about organizational noise.**

   The value of organizational input is obvious: by listening, we gain crucial insight, but that doesn't mean we need to listen to all the noise.

   We can learn from those on the ground, the very people who are facing the battle every day. Although they may have insight, they may also be wrong. They have a slanted view of day-to-day activities based on current emotional pain and their organizational point of view. It is important for our team members to understand that they should not base their long-term plans on short-term emotional pain, which is likely to induce a knee-jerk reaction.

   A development discussion allows the leader to demonstrate a balance between signal and noise.

2. **We can learn from those who have had different experiences in the past.**

   Let's face it: experience matters! The things people have done in the past are legitimate, concrete situations they can point to and say, "See? This is what happens when you..." And yet, if we simply rely on those who have had a bad experience, we are likely to be pulled by the emotional tug of a wounded victim. As leaders, we can point people toward others with vast experience who can share how they solved a problem in the past. Everyone wins. This kind of development discussion eases the fear some employees have when they contact an expert in the organization who is "always right" and does not like to be challenged.

3. We can learn from our peers who have done similar projects.

I find this group to be the most effective of the bunch, simply because they've had to navigate tough waters in the same organization, yet even they may have a somewhat jaded view of the situation, simply because they led a different team or their own leadership methods were ineffective. *(Not all leaders are equal.)*

4. Be cautious of overdependence on technology.

Technology reigns supreme these days in most circles. Ignoring the techies of the world is not wise. People with good technical sense can make the world a better place, but technology for the sake of technology is never a good idea. Still, there are those who want to try every new thing that hits the cloud! Balancing tech costs with tech efficiencies is a great exercise in a development discussion.

So how do we help our team members develop in the context of all this noise?

1. A great starting point is to remind a team member that no one, and I mean no one, has *the* complete solution to any organizational problem or challenge. As a leader, it's your job to coach your team members to weigh all perspectives and build a solution.

2. It's good to explain to our team members that we should *listen to those who are truly interested in our success*—people who have a track record of investing in our careers, those who want us to succeed.

3. Remind them to always listen for the real kernel of truth from those who are most frustrated. *Somewhere in their rant is a legitimate warning.*

4. Teach team members that their decisions and approach will not make everyone happy. It just won't happen. Validating them when they have been dissed by other managers goes a long way to strengthen the bond between you. Of course, you need to be careful about expressing too much negativity about another manager. It's bad modeling and can backfire.

A Personal Story

Early in my first supervisory role, I had a conversation with my boss. I told him I was going to talk to everyone about a decision I made to make sure everyone would like it. He was a little irritated that I had taken the time to try and ensure everyone would be happy with my decision, knowing that my decision was not likely to please everyone.

He asked me, *"Have you thought this through?"*

I answered, "Yes."

"Have you considered the different angles of your decision?"

Again, I answered, "Yes."

"Have you done your best?"

"Yes," I replied.

He answered: *"Then you need to move forward with your decision."*

At the end of the day, no leader will be right all the time, and while we need not ignore people, we must ignore the noise. That's an important lesson to share with our team members as we help them develop.

What steps have you taken to explain how you think about problems or processes?

What will be your biggest personal challenge explaining how you think about organizational problems and issues?

CHAPTER 10 SYNOPSIS

Teaching people *how we think* is an incredibly valuable development activity. It's worth taking the time to teach people our approach to problem solving. The Cognitive Apprenticeship model clarifies how to approach this element of development. **It simply means expressing how we think about how we think!**

CHAPTER 11

LEADERSHIP IS MORE THAN A JOB

WORKING DEFINITION

People Development is the process of

(1) gaining new knowledge,

(2) learning new skills,

(3) improving efficacy,

(4) strengthening existing capabilities, and

(5) gaining achievements that validate someone's value in the organization.

Leaders have long been in need of a set of guidelines and principles to develop people. By reading this book, you now have a deeper and clearer picture of processes and insights to improve your employee development activities.

We've looked at the need for development, written a definition, evaluated a rationale for development, studied how motivation can be activated during development, evaluated both shallow and deep-water development, and considered the key behavior of leadership patience. We've identified and addressed some of the objections to development, evaluated the process, and considered the wide variety of development opportunities available to leaders and managers, including cognitive apprenticeship. We studied the roles of both leaders and employees in the development process, along with need for strong organizational support. We've learned that development has benefits for the employee, the organization, and the leader.

Having read this book, you now know the subject is deeper and more multifaceted than most leaders realize.

Development of others tells us that *leadership is more than a job.* Leadership is an opportunity to give people satisfying careers through development opportunities. Isn't it fascinating that as managers we can truly change lives by developing people? As Elizabeth Thelen says, "We *get* to do this."

We can make long-term changes in people's lives while accomplishing organizational goals. Development engages the motivations and energies of others in a way that simple day-to-day, check-the-box management just doesn't.

People development creates energy and activates motivation. People find themselves enriched by new projects and significant challenges AND when they accomplish something, they become *more confident* and seek out *greater challenges*. That's good for you as a leader, it's good for the team, the individual and the organization!

People know if you're on *their* team and want *them* to succeed, and their productivity is influenced by your interest in their careers. Increasing their productivity strengthens the entire team, and in so doing, the organization gets stronger by retaining the best team members.

Developing someone can have a long-term impact over a lifetime. We may never see the full value of the work we've done to develop someone, but we can find deep satisfaction in helping others achieve their career success along the way. In other words, *there's more to this job than a job.*

People development is key for retention. There is no current theory of development. My hope is that this book spurs some deeper research and analysis into the subject of development. There are several academic angles that I'm sure would yield rich findings in a structured scholarly environment, which could benefit practitioners and organizations around the world. HR teams, in particular, could benefit from a deeper dive into effective development. The next generation of team members has high expectations that their leaders will be skilled developers of human talent. There's more research to be done.

After decades of working with and managing teams, it is deeply gratifying to hear the following phrase from team members I have served: "You were one of the good ones."

Ultimately, people development requires an attitude of delight in the success of others. As a leader, you can make that choice and impact your people right now and for the rest of their careers.

And maybe for the rest of their lives.
So go and develop others,
because leadership is more than a job!

APPENDIX A

The #1 Phrase to Avoid when Developing People

There is a phrase that has serious drawbacks when an employee may react to a development opportunity. Using this phrase has significant consequences.

"You're not a team player."

While it is never wise to question the motives of others, it is safe (and fair) to consider the impact of the phrase, since in a corporate context, it may be one of the most manipulative strings of words in the English language.

Here are some of the implications:

- You're obviously not willing to help us all succeed.
- You're obviously in this for your own gain.
- You're not thinking of the bigger picture.
- You're not interested in our success.

It is a crushing phrase that immediately puts someone on the defensive. As soon as that happens, we're on the ropes, and with a flushed face of embarrassment, we begin explaining that we are indeed willing to help, willing to be part of something, willing to see the team succeed. (Meanwhile, in the back of our minds, we know we don't have the resources, span of control, time, funding, or extra hands to complete the task we've been challenged with.)

Those who use the phrase know exactly what they're doing. They are putting people in the uncomfortable position of having to commit to something out of sheer guilt and fear of a loss of reputation. In some cases, I believe it borders on organizational extortion and in others, psychological abuse. ***It is of no value in the development process.***

If you've been a target of this questionable phrase, consider whether this is a consistent method of the person's managerial tactics. If so, others know, because they've experienced the same tactic.

Be diplomatic but direct: "My track record demonstrates a consistently high level of support for this organization, and we'll do what needs to be done, but let me offer that this project stands in the way of several other major corporate initiatives. Just so I'm clear, what's the priority?"

If you've used this questionable phrase, rethink your approach. There are far better ways to gain team member collaboration without resorting to manipulative pressure. Only weak leaders turn to this type of tactic. Over the long run, your reputation will precede you and people will come to expect this sort of behavior. This phrase is sophomoric, at best. Embarrassing team members into cooperation may work in the short term, but over the long haul, you'll build resentment and lose key people.

And you'll build a reputation as someone who uses pressure instead of influence to get the job done.

APPENDIX B

Virtual Development

Clearly, the post-COVID world has changed our options for employee development. As leaders, we're already aware of the challenges posed by virtual team members. But that doesn't leave us off the hook for development.

Connecting with people through Zoom is a start, but nothing beats getting on a plane and meeting someone face-to-face even for a few hours to make an emotional connection that can be extended through online contact. When I had a team in Europe, I met with them face-to-face, then continued to work daily to ensure they had the support they needed. That meant some early meetings at times.

One thing is certain: regular contact with a virtual person is essential during a development project, and it is even more important to *have someone local available if something goes wrong,* especially if your team member is in another time zone and another part of the world.

Above all, don't forget that virtual people are flags flying in the wind, often alone without support. Your investment of time in development will give them a sense of belonging.

Adult Learning:
The Framework for Development and Behavior Change

Much of what we call development is gaining new experiences, also known as Adult Learning. As leaders, it's worth our time to consider how to make an experience stick. In other words, what learning will remain once the development experience is completed? Understanding the principles of adult learning is beneficial in developing others, because by considering each element you can improve on the way you create and select development experiences. This chart will guide you through the different elements of Adult Learning.

CATEGORY OF CHANGE	RANGE OF CHANGE EXPERIENCE — Dr. Jim Bohn
IMPACT	Mere Sensory Impressions 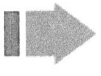 Change Retention, Memory
SITUATIONAL #1	Familiar Situations Novel Situations
SITUATIONAL #2	Meaningless Situations Meaningful Situations
MEMORY	① Transformation Of Energy ② Selective Perception ③ Working Memory ④ Long Term Memory
COGNITIVE KNOWLEDGE COMPONENT	Semantic/Declarative Knowledge — Procedural Processing
KNOWLEDGE CATEGORIES	Data, Facts  Rules of Thumb
PHYSICAL (NEUROLOGICAL) LEVEL	Little or No Change In connections between neurons  Extensive Change In Connections between neurons
WAY TO DESCRIBE CHANGE EXPERIENCE	① Things that don't stick "day-to-day" Routine ② Things that change us for a while ③ Things that change us permanently

The goal of a development experience is retention.

The chart shows several ways to look at a developmental experience. Here are some questions to ask yourself as you engage an employee in development.

1. Does the situation have a deep impact on us or is it just a passing impression?

2. Is the situation familiar? If so, there is likely little opportunity for development. New things create interest and cause us to pay attention.

3. Is the situation meaningful? In other words, does this experience have some value for the person, or is it simply marking time?

4. The cognitive element of experience is a bit more complex, but it simply means, "Did my brain assess a situation, put it into working memory and then transform me over the long haul?"

5. Is the development experience about data, new facts? Or is it about learning a new process. These are two different kinds of learning.

6. One of the reasons people struggle with change is because a physical transformation takes place in the brain when people adjust to new things. This can even cause physical headaches or stress. Experience directly impacts the neurons in the brain.

7. So we see a development activity is part of a range of stuff we see every day, to things that change us for a while. Think of a motivational speech that excites us, then quickly fades. But some things change us permanently and become part of our behavioral repertoire.

Bandura, Albert. Self-Efficacy: The Exercise of Control-W. H. Freeman & Co (1997)

Collins, A., Brown, J. S., & Newman, S. E. (1987). Cognitive apprenticeship: Teaching the craft of reading, writing and mathematics (Technical Report No. 403). BBN Laboratories, Cambridge, MA. Centre for the Study of Reading, University of Illinois. January 1987.

Ghefaili, A., Journal of Educational Computing, Design & Online learning Volume 4, Fall, 2003 Cognitive Apprenticeship, Technology, and the Contextualization of Learning Environments 1 Cognitive Apprenticeship, Technology, and the Contextualization of Learning Environments

Harter, J. K., Schmidt, F. L., & Hayes, T. L. (2002). Business-unit-level relationship between employee satisfaction, employee engagement, and business outcomes: A meta-analysis. Journal of applied psychology, 87(2), 268-279. https://doi.org/10.1037/0021-9010.87.2.268

Kahn, W. A. (1990). Psychological conditions of personal engagement and disengagement at work. Academy of management journal, 33(4), 692-724.

To date, there is no theory of employee development, so this subject required a well-rounded set of viewpoints to produce a thorough evaluation of the subject. I engaged with seasoned senior executives, academics, training practitioners, technical experts, HR experts, healthcare leaders, operations leads, and consultants to gain their insights. Collectively they've worked with thousands of people and hundreds of leaders. Although there are some themes common to all who provided their perspectives, they also each see the topic of development a bit differently because of their experience and the diverse environments they serve. I wanted to gain the best insights to ensure the book was thorough and impacted a wide range of organizational leaders.

I am humbled by the many people who have contributed their insight into this book, including:

Christine Bakewicz, Director, Training and Development, United Health Group, Minneapolis. She made several significant suggestions that changed the book for the better! Thanks so much, Christine!

Kerry Brunner, VP, Benefits Ascension Healthcare. Thank you for focusing on the interaction between employee and leader and virtual development.

Patrick Cline, Ph.D. Liberty University Adjunct, Business Professor, Organizational Psychologist, Change Management Professional. Thanks for being a wise thinker and a good friend.

Jay Held, retired VP, training and development, offered strategic views of the development process. Grateful for your help and insights through the years.

Barry Keller, executive and CEO. You read a very early draft and gave me significant encouragement!

Glenn Kormanik, CEO, Zero Zone. You were one of the first to read an early draft and your executive experience was instrumental in my approach to several sections.

Carrie Lauersdorf, Engineer. Thanks for providing the perspective of how technical people experience development and for your recommendations on the cover!

Mike Markiewicz, Executive Director, LUBAR School of Business, Milwaukee. Of all the customers I have ever served, Mike is at the top of the list. He read an early draft and pointed out some areas for improvement and added some great quotes.

James Mylett, Senior Vice-President, Schneider Electric, a friend and colleague for many years at Johnson Controls, offered encouragement and an executive's viewpoint. James is a leader's leader and has been an inspiration to me for many years.

Monte Pedersen, Principal of the CDA Group, LLC, is a colleague who continues to support me with useful organizational advice based in his decades of experience.

Suzanne Sherry, MBA, Human Capital Consulting Consultant and Former VP of Employee Development, gave me some early insights into development. With an abundance of professional and experiential advice over a cup of coffee, she helped me get the project started. This is her area of expertise, so I listened closely! Her guidance and friendship is much appreciated!

Dr. Wilma Slenders, MSM, PCC, Consultant. Thank you for a thorough analysis of an early draft. Her insight helped clarify a few ideas and her overview pointed out some areas to increase consistency in the text. She also provided some research that supported concepts in the book.

Elizabeth Thelen, M.S., Executive Director, Technology Park, Whitewater University. Business Coach, **Be Do Have Share** Services, HR Consultant, and longtime friend. Your experience with scores of leaders and different markets adds much depth to the book.

Kim Thelen, Senior Director of Global Accounts, CBRE. Kim was on my team for many years and has gone on to be a superstar in business!

Michelle Wendt, Trainer, Lawrence Livermore Laboratories, California, offered several early suggestions that guided my thinking.

Jim Bohn, Ph.D.

PEOPLE DEVELOPMENT

Jim Bohn, Ph.D.

Jim Bohn, Ph.D.

Jim Bohn, Ph.D.

Jim Bohn, Ph.D.